P9-DGI-912

cocktails

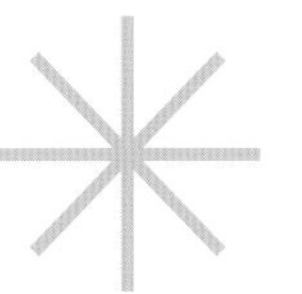

p

This is a Parragon Publishing Book
First published in 2006

Parragon Publishing
Queen Street House
4 Queen Street
Bath BA1 1HE, UK

Designed, produced, and packaged by Fiona Roberts
Edited by Julie Whitaker and Ian Whitelaw

ISBN: 1-40548-301-6

Printed in China

WARNING

Recipes containing raw eggs are not suitable for children, convalescents, the elderly, or pregnant women. Please consume alcohol responsibly. Participation in the games and activities described in this book, and the related consumption of alcoholic drinks, is entirely the responsibility of the individual, and neither the author, the publishers, nor their agents can accept liability for such participation or consumption, or the rules, procedure, or outcome of any game contained herein. All consumption of alcohol is entirely at the participant's own risk.

Measuring the quantities is one of the keys to a good cocktail. The standard single measure is 1 fluid ounce, as used in this book, and you can buy stainless steel measures (jiggers) for 1, 2, and ½ quantities in many department stores. However, like any good bartender, you can use your own chosen measure as long as you follow the proportions given in the recipes. An appropriately small tumbler, glass, or even eggcup will serve as the basic measure. A dash is four or five drops—just enough to add a little color or taste.

cocktails

Cocktail Chic

Cocktail parties are firmly back on the map—in fact, they never really went away. From the heyday of 1920s flappers and 1950s Hollywood glam, to Sex-And-The-City style **über-chic** gatherings, cocktail parties have an unmistakable charm. Cocktails are famed for their versatility and sense of occasion. You can serve cocktails and canapés as a prelude to a dinner party, or simply mix a few **cocktails with friends** before you go out for dinner or drinks. Alternatively, you could host a short **"happy hour"** gathering after work to let go and celebrate the weekend!

Cocktail parties can be casual yet trendy, or simply downright sophisticated. Once the idea for a full-blown party takes root, you will soon realize that cocktails can take you almost anywhere—**parties** can even be themed for a big event or special occasion. Dress codes or **themed food and music** are also great fun.

The focus of the cocktail party is **entertainment** and experimentation. Your guests can try a variety of drinks and it doesn't matter if they don't like one in particular as there's always another cocktail on its way! Here are a few tips to ensure your party goes with a swing.

getting the party started

⁜ The perfect food for cocktail parties is finger food. Keep it simple and you can't go wrong. You can buy pre-prepared canapés or you could make a few dishes yourself in advance. These days you don't need to fall back on sausage rolls or cheese and pineapple on a stick—why not try tapas or sushi instead?

⁜ Make some space in the kitchen and dust off your cocktail shaker. Try to clear your kitchen counters so that people have room to make their concoctions. Have a cloth or paper towels ready for those inevitable spillages.

- Make sure you have enough glasses. Try to provide different style glasses for the various cocktails, including wine glasses, straight-sided highball glasses for tall drinks, tumblers for spirits and juices, shot glasses, and martini glasses. No plastic glasses!
- Don't forget the little details—olives, salt, sugar, stirrer, cocktail umbrellas, lemons, orange twists, and candied cherries.
- Essential spirits include vodka, rum, gin, scotch, bourbon, blended whiskey, and tequila. If your budget allows, consider stocking Kahlúa, crème de menthe, Amaretto, brandy and/or cognac, Grand Marnier, and Drambuie.
- Don't forget essential mixers—orange juice, soda, tonic, ginger ale, cola, tomato juice, Tabasco sauce, Worcestershire sauce, and, of course, lots of ice!
- So you've brought the drinks, set out the canapés, and invited your guests; which cocktails would you like to try? The centerpiece of the party has to be the **"Classic Cocktails"**. Why not create a "menu" for the evening by picking out your top five classics? Shots are always popular at a party in full swing, and our next chapter, **"Shooters,"** is dedicated to these short and sassy treats. Not all the fun is reserved for the alcoholic drinks, and in **"Angelic Delights"** you can discover the pleasures of non-alcoholic cocktails. These are perfect for an afternoon barbecue or family function—and the designated drivers will be delighted! No sophisticated dinner party is complete without an after-dinner tipple, and **"Fine Finales"** provides classic drinks as well as contemporary variations. From Irish Coffee to Port and Lemon Mull, there's a recipe for the perfect final drink for every guest.

To accompany these fabulous cocktails, you can find a selection of hilarious drinking games throughout the book, and I'm sure we don't need to say, always make sure you drink responsibly. Have fun!

classic cocktails

This chapter is full of style and flair, with classic cocktails including Pimm's No.1, Pina Colada, and the fabulous Long Island Iced Tea. Every party needs a drop of something special, and after browsing these pages you'll never be short of the perfect drink!

Tequila Sunrise

serves 1 ⁘ 2 measures silver tequila ⁘ cracked ice cubes ⁘ orange juice ⁘ 1 measure grenadine

This is one cocktail you shouldn't rush when making, or you will spoil the attractive sunrise effect produced by the grenadine slowly spreading through the orange juice.

- Pour the tequila over cracked ice in a chilled highball glass and top up with the orange juice.
- Stir well to mix.
- Slowly pour in the grenadine and serve with a straw.

Mimosa

serves 1

- fresh orange juice
- 2 measures champagne, chilled

The original of this drink was invariably made with Bollinger champagne, and it is true that the better the quality of the champagne, the better the flavor.

Half fill a chilled flute with the orange juice, then gently pour in the chilled champagne.

Manhattan

serves 1 ⁂ 4–6 cracked ice cubes ⁂ dash of Angostura bitters ⁂ 3 measures rye whiskey ⁂ 1 measure sweet vermouth

to decorate ⁂ cocktail cherry

Said to have been invented by Sir Winston Churchill's American mother, Jennie, the Manhattan is one of many cocktails named after places in New York.

- Put the cracked ice cubes into a mixing glass. Dash the Angostura bitters over the ice and pour in the whiskey and vermouth. Stir well to mix.
- Strain into a chilled glass and decorate with a cocktail cherry.

Pina Colada

serves 1 ⁂ 4–6 crushed ice cubes ⁂ 2 measures white rum ⁂ 1 measure dark rum ⁂ 3 measures pineapple juice ⁂ 2 measures coconut cream

to decorate ⁂ pineapple wedges

One of the younger generation of classics, this became popular during the cocktail revival of the 1980s and has remained so ever since.

- Whizz the crushed ice in a blender with the white rum, dark rum, pineapple juice, and coconut cream until smooth.
- Pour, without straining, into a tall chilled glass and dress with pineapple wedges.

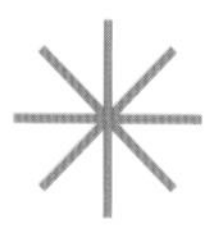

Margarita

serves 1 ⁂ 4–6 cracked ice cubes ⁂ 3 measures white tequila ⁂ 1 measure Triple Sec ⁂ 2 measures lime juice

to decorate ⁂ wedge of lime ⁂ coarse salt ⁂ slice of lime

This cocktail, attributed to Francisco Morales and invented in 1942 in Mexico, is a more civilized version of the original way to drink tequila–a lick of salt from the back of the hand, a shot of tequila, and a suck of lime juice!

- Rub the rim of a chilled cocktail glass with the lime wedge and then dip in a saucer of coarse salt to frost.
- Put the cracked ice cubes into a cocktail shaker. Pour the tequila, Triple Sec, and lime juice over the ice. Shake vigorously until a frost forms.
- Strain into the prepared glass and decorate with a slice of lime.

Daiquiri

serves 1 ⁂ 2 measures white rum ⁂ ¾ measure lime juice ⁂ ½ tsp sugar syrup ⁂ cracked ice

Daiquiri is a town in Cuba, where this drink was said to have been invented in the early part of the 20th century. A businessman had run out of imported gin and so had to make do with the local drink—rum—which, at that time, was often of unreliable quality.

- Pour the rum, lime juice, and sugar syrup over ice and shake vigorously until well frosted.
- Strain into a chilled cocktail glass.

Bloody Mary

serves 1 ⁂ dash Worcestershire sauce ⁂ dash Tabasco sauce ⁂ cracked ice cubes ⁂ 2 measures vodka ⁂ splash dry sherry ⁂ 6 measures tomato juice ⁂ juice of half a lemon ⁂ pinch celery salt ⁂ pinch cayenne pepper

to decorate ⁂ slice of lemon ⁂ celery stalk with leaves

This classic cocktail was invented in 1921 at the legendary Harry's Bar in Paris. There are numerous versions—some much hotter and spicier. Ingredients may include horseradish sauce in addition to, or instead of, Tabasco sauce.

- Dash the Worcestershire sauce and Tabasco sauce over ice in a shaker and add the vodka, sherry, tomato juice, and lemon juice.
- Shake vigorously until frosted.
- Strain into a tall chilled glass, add a pinch of celery salt and a pinch of cayenne, and decorate with a celery stalk and a slice of lemon.

Long Island Iced Tea

serves 2 ⁜ 2 measures vodka ⁜ 1 measure gin ⁜ 1 measure white tequila ⁜ 1 measure white rum ⁜ ½ measure white crème de menthe ⁜ 2 measures lemon juice ⁜ 1 tsp sugar syrup ⁜ cracked ice cubes ⁜ cola

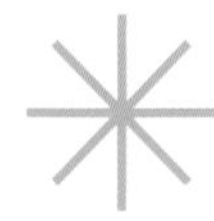

to decorate ⁜ wedge of lime or lemon

Dating back to Prohibition days, when it was drunk out of cups in an attempt to convince the FBI that it was harmless, this cocktail has evolved from the original simple combination of vodka with a dash of cola!

- Shake the vodka, gin, tequila, rum, crème de menthe, lemon juice, and sugar syrup vigorously over ice until well frosted.
- Strain into ice-filled highball glasses and top up with cola.
- Dress with lime or lemon wedges.

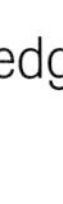

Harvey Wallbanger

serves 1 ⁑ 3 measures vodka ⁑ 8 measures orange juice ⁑ 2 tsp Galliano ⁑ ice cubes

to decorate ⁑ cocktail cherry and a slice of orange

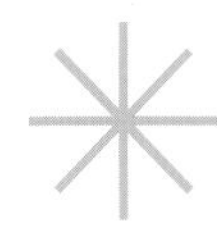

This well-known contemporary classic cocktail is a great party drink—mix it strong at first, then weaker as the evening goes by. Leave out the alcohol for drivers and no one will know!

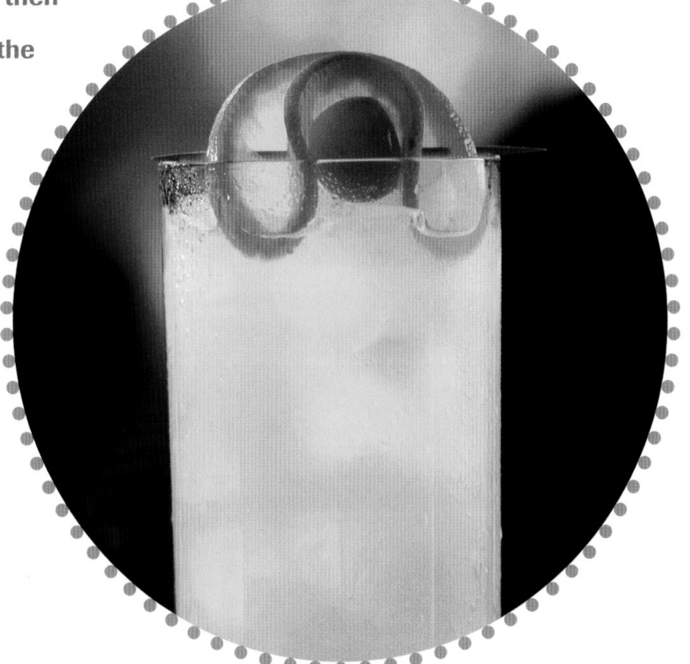

- Half fill a highball glass with ice, pour vodka and orange juice over the ice cubes, and float Galliano on top.
- Garnish with a cherry and a slice of orange.
- For a warming variant, mix a splash of ginger wine with the vodka and orange.

Martini

serves 1 ⁑ 3 measures gin ⁑ 1 tsp dry vermouth, or to taste ⁑ cracked ice cubes

to decorate ⁑ green pitted olive

For many, this is the ultimate cocktail. It is named after its inventor, Martini de Anna de Toggia, not the famous brand of vermouth!

- Pour the gin and vermouth over cracked ice in a mixing glass and stir well to mix.
- Strain into a chilled martini glass and decorate with a green olive.

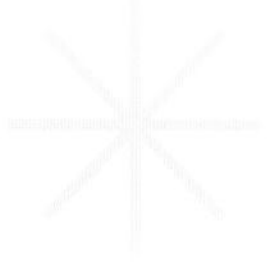

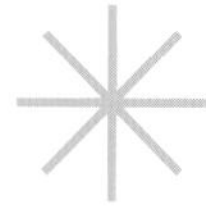

Pimm's No.1

serves 1 ⁂ ice ⁂ 1 measure Pimm's ⁂ lemonade

to decorate ⁂ slices of orange and lemon ⁂ strips of cucumber peel, sprigs of mint

Pimm's No. 1 is a long, deliciously dry but fruity concoction, with a gin base flavored with herbs. It was devised by James Pimm, a London restaurateur, in the late 19th century and was quite probably the original gin sling.

- Fill a large chilled glass two-thirds full with ice and pour in the Pimm's.
- Top up with lemonade and stir gently.
- Decorate with a strip of cucumber peel, a sprig of fresh mint, and slices of orange and lemon.

Mai Tai

serves 2 ⁂ 2 measures white rum ⁂ 2 measures dark rum ⁂ 1 measure orange Curaçao ⁂ 1 measure lime juice ⁂ 1 tbsp orgeat ⁂ 1 tbsp grenadine ⁂ cracked ice cubes

to decorate ⁂ slices of pineapple and pieces of fruit peel, cocktail cherries, and straws

Created in 1944 by restaurateur "Trader Vic," it was described as "Mai Tai–Roe Ae" meaning "out of this world." It is always flamboyantly dressed.

- Shake the white and dark rums, Curaçao, lime juice, orgeat, and grenadine vigorously over ice until well frosted.
- Strain into chilled Collins glasses and decorate as you wish.

Drinking Games

The Rhyming Game

Number of players: 4+

You will need: No special equipment.

How to play:

✻ One of the group says a word, any word that has rhyming potential. The next player then has to come up with a word that rhymes with it… and so on around the circle. As the game progresses, players try to introduce more difficult words with which to rhyme.

✻ If a player says a word that doesn't rhyme with the previous one, or repeats a word, or hesitates for too long, she must take a drink. The next player then starts a new round with a new word.

✻ There are also drink penalties for foreign words, proper nouns (names of people or places), acronyms, and slang, none of which is permitted.

Soap Spotting

Number of players: 4–10

You will need: A television during a scheduled soap opera transmission, or videos/DVDs of your favorite soaps.

How to play:

✼ Soaps are nothing if not repetitious. The idea of this game is to take a drink whenever certain regular incidents, major or minor, happen on screen. These highly predictable soap events are agreed beforehand by all the players, with different categories incurring different drinking penalties.

✼ For example:

Everyone takes a drink whenever:

- Two characters kiss.
- A character storms out of a room.
- A character cries.
- There is someone at the door.
- Someone takes a drink.

✼ Everyone takes two drinks whenever any of the following appear:

- A cop (in uniform or plain clothes).
- A taxi driver.
- A member of the clergy (any denomination).
- A hospital nurse.
- A cat or a dog.

✼ Everyone takes three drinks whenever:

- There's a car crash or someone has an accident.
- A crime is committed.
- A couple splits up.
- A character gives birth.
- Someone dies.

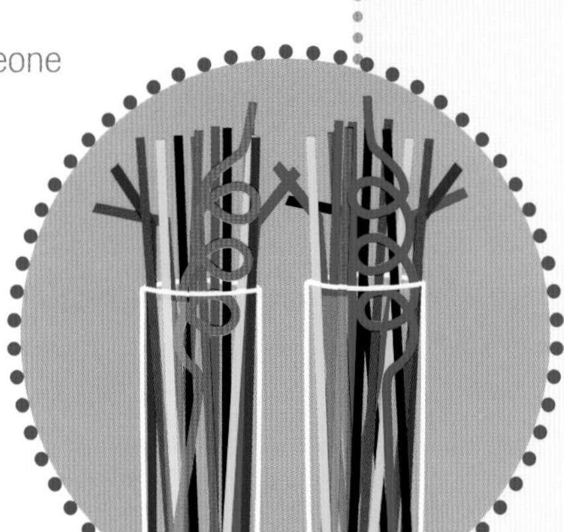

Musical Chairs

Number of players: 10+

You will need: 10 chairs or stools that can be easily maneuvered into two rows, back to back, and some recorded music.

How to play:

❊ The game is basically the same as that played at children's parties, except with the added and vital dimension of alcohol.

❊ Everyone sits on a chair, one per person. The music starts and the players get up and dance in a circular direction around the chairs, one of which is then removed.

❊ When the music stops everyone dashes for a chair and sits down. Except, that is, for the player left standing, who is now out of the game and incurs a two-drink penalty.

❊ The process is then repeated until just two people remain circling one chair. The player who secures the chair when the music finally stops is the winner.

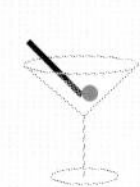

Guess Who

Number of players: 6-10

You will need: A blindfold.

How to play:

❋ An adult variation of the children's game, Blind Man's Buff.

❋ One of the group is blindfolded and taken to one side. A second player is then "disguised" by putting on extra apparel or by exchanging clothes with someone else.

❋ The blindfolded person is brought alongside and has one minute in which to identify the targeted individual by touch.

❋ If the blindfolded person fails to identify the target within the allotted time, she must have a drink and another player is then selected to put on the blindfold.

❋ If the blindfolded person guesses the identity of the target, everyone else must have a drink and it is the targeted individual who wears the blindfold next.

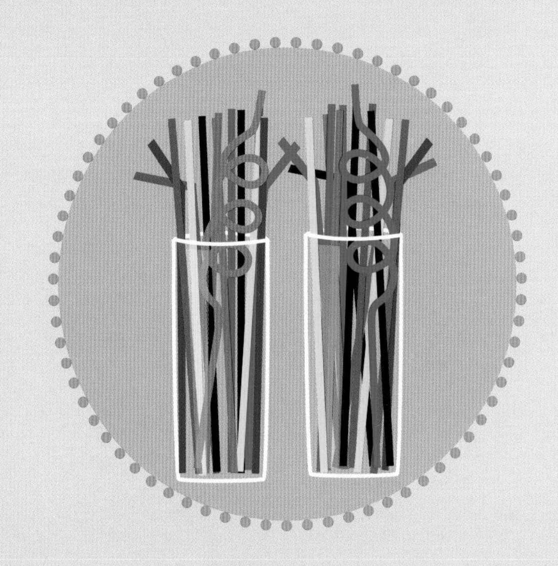

shooters

Love them or hate them, shooters are the perfect way to really kick-start a party. Sample some of these delicious cocktails and you may be surprised to find how tasty they can be. Be a devil and try a Russian Double, an exotic Peach Floyd, or a good old Tequila Shot!

Russian Double

serves 1 ⁑ 1 measure red vodka, iced ⁑ strips of lemon or orange peel
⁑ 1 measure lemon vodka or schnapps, iced

Vodka and schnapps are both very strong drinks, so handle with care!

Layer the drinks carefully in a chilled shot glass, putting a strip of peel in the first layer, and drink immediately.

Napoleon's Nightcap

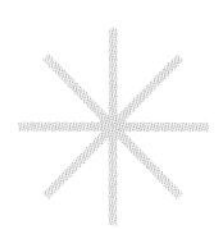

serves 1 ⁑ $1\frac{1}{4}$ measures cognac ⁑ 1 measure dark crème de cacao ⁑ $\frac{1}{4}$ measure crème de banane ⁑ 1 tbsp heavy cream

Instead of hot chocolate at bedtime, Napoleon apparently favored a chocolate-laced brandy with a hint of banana. Daring and extravagant!

- Stir the first three ingredients in a mixing glass with ice.
- Strain into a chilled glass and spoon on a layer of cream.

Whiskey Mac

serves 1 ⁜ $1\frac{1}{2}$ measures Scotch whiskey ⁜ 1 measure ginger wine

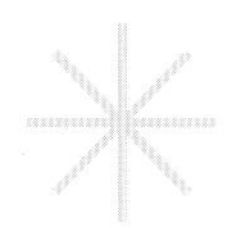

This popular classic is enjoyed worldwide as a warming winter drink, so don't be tempted to chill the glass or the drinks.

⁜ Carefully pour the ingredients into an old-fashioned glass and allow to mix but don't stir.

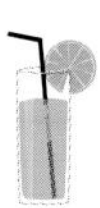

Chilly Willy

serves 1 ⁑ 2 measures vodka ⁑ 1 tsp chopped fresh chile ⁑ cracked ice cubes

Truly a cocktail for the brave-hearted—the heat depends on the type of chile (some are much more fiery than others) as well as the quantity you add and whether the chile was seeded (most of the heat resides in the seeds) first. For an even spicier cocktail, use chile vodka as well!

- Shake the vodka over ice with the chile until a frost forms.
- Strain into a small chilled tumbler.

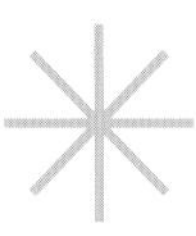

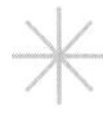

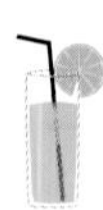

Hair of the Dog

serves 1 ⁕ 1 measure Scotch whiskey ⁕ 1 1/2 measures light cream ⁕ 1/2 measure clear honey

This well-known expression—a tot of whatever gave you the hangover in the first place—is in fact a popular Scottish "morning after" tipple!

- Gently mix the whiskey, cream, and honey together.
- Pour into a cocktail glass over ice and down it.

Peach Floyd

serves 1 ⁜ 1 measure peach schnapps, chilled ⁜ 1 measure vodka, chilled ⁜ 1 measure white cranberry and peach juice, chilled ⁜ 1 measure cranberry juice, chilled

Shots of this cocktail look stunning in the right type of glass, but as they are for drinking down in one, keep them small and have everything really well chilled.

Stir all the ingredients together over ice and pour into an iced shot glass.

Tequila Shot

serves 1 ⁘ pinch salt ⁘ 1 measure gold tequila

to decorate ⁘ wedge of lime

According to custom, this is the only way to drink neat tequila. It is often described as being smooth and tart, so adding lime juice and salt may sound contradictory, but it works!

- Pour the tequila into a shot glass.
- Put the salt at the base of your thumb, between thumb and forefinger.
- Hold the lime wedge in the same hand.
- Hold the shot in the other hand.
- Lick the salt, down the tequila, and suck the lime.

Dandy

serves 1 ⁜ 1/2 measure rye whiskey ⁜ 1/2 measure Dubonnet ⁜ dash Angostura bitters ⁜ 3 dashes cassis ⁜ ice

to decorate ⁜ few frozen berries

The fruit flavor is what gives this rich combination a special touch.

- Mix the first four ingredients with ice and strain into an iced shot glass.
- Dress with a berry or two.

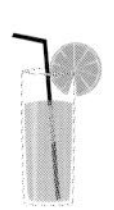

Tornado

serves 1

- 1 measure peach or other favorite schnapps, frozen
- 1 measure black Sambuca, frozen

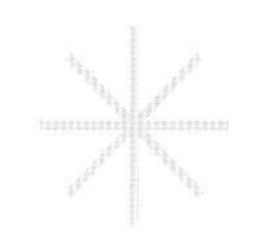

If the liqueurs are really well iced, you will certainly create a tornado in your glass when you pour one into the other—just sit and watch them swirling for a moment!

- Pour the schnapps into an iced shot glass.
- Gently pour on the Sambuca over the back of a spoon.
- Leave for a few minutes to settle and separate before you down it.

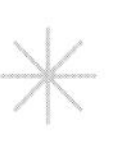

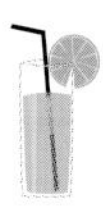

Silver Berry

serves 1 ⁑ 1 measure raspberry vodka, iced ⁑ 1 measure crème de cassis, iced ⁑ 1 measure Cointreau, iced

to decorate ⁑ edible silver paper or a frozen berry

This drink is perfect for one of those very special occasions—except that you really can't drink very many!

- Carefully and slowly layer the three liqueurs in the order listed, in a well-iced shot glass or a tall thin cocktail glass.
- The liqueurs must be well iced first and may need time to settle into their layers.
- Decorate with the silver paper or a frozen berry.

Anouchka

serves 1 ⁑ 1 measure vodka, iced ⁑ dash black Sambuca. ⁑ dash crème de mure

to decorate ⁑ a few blackberries

Sambuca is licorice flavored and therefore not to everyone's taste. However, used here with a dash of blackberry liqueur and a measure of iced vodka, it helps create a great combination.

- Pour the vodka into a chilled shot glass.
- Add a dash of Sambuca and then a dash of crème de mure.
- Dress with a few blackberries, fresh or frozen.

Jockey Club Special

serves 1 ⁕ 1 measure gin ⁕ ½ measure crème de noyaux ⁕ good splash lemon juice ⁕ 2 dashes orange bitters ⁕ 2 dashes Angostura bitters ⁕ ice

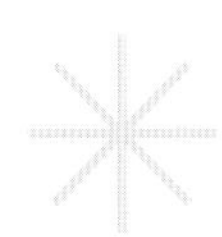

A short cocktail with a good kick in its tail, but you can mellow it by serving on the rocks if you prefer!

Stir all the ingredients well over ice and strain into a cocktail glass.

I Never Ever Have

Number of players: 6–10

You will need: No special equipment.

How to play:

❋ This is a great game for a group of close friends to play, as they can share intimate secrets about each other. It is also a fun way of getting to know people.

❋ Everyone sits around a table or in a circle on the floor. One person starts by making a true statement that begins with the words "I never ever have." For example, "I never ever have cheated in an exam."

If any other player has cheated in an exam, or whatever the claim is, she must raise her hand and have a drink. No explanation is required, no questions asked.

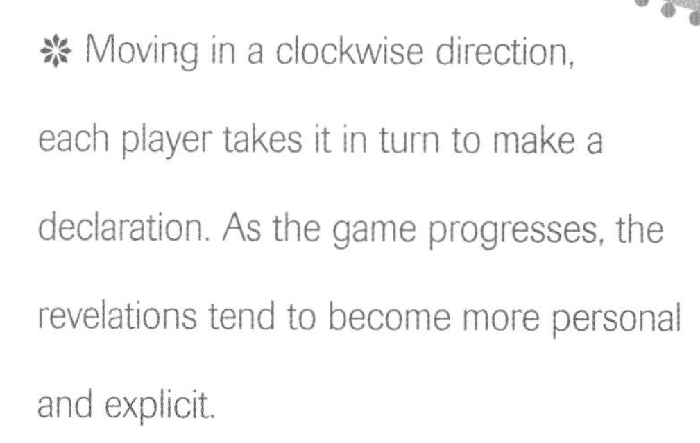

❋ Moving in a clockwise direction, each player takes it in turn to make a declaration. As the game progresses, the revelations tend to become more personal and explicit.

❋ The game works best if people are strictly honest in their declarations and responses. It is amazing what you can learn about your friends.

I'm a Celebrity

Number of players: 4+

You will need: No special equipment.

How to play:

❋ The challenge is to imitate a well-known person, past or present, without uttering a single, solitary word. You can mime their walk or posture, make hand gestures and facial expressions, and use an appropriate prop if there is one handy. But you are not allowed to speak. You can, incidentally, be a famous cartoon character, like one of the Simpsons, if you think you can manage it.

❋ The other players have to identify your celebrity. They are not permitted to ask questions and can only have one shot each at the answer. You must continue to perform your celebrity routine until they have all had a guess, or until someone has identified you.

❋ Every wrong guess incurs a drink penalty for the incorrect guesser. If someone guesses correctly, the "celebrity" must have a drink. If, by common consent, the performance was nothing like the celebrity in question, the player miming the role must empty her glass.

❋ Then it's time for the next celebrity.

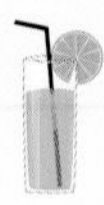

Spoof

Number of players: 2+ (the more, the merrier)

You will need: Three coins per player.

How to play:

❋ Each player conceals up to three coins (0, 1, 2, or 3) in her clenched fist, without disclosing how many she has selected—if any at all. All the players then hold out their fists, with their contents still hidden.

❋ Taking it in turns, each player has to guess the total number of coins contained in all the fists. No two players can opt for guessing the same number in any one round.

❋ The player who guesses the correct number of coins wins, and then drops out of the game. As a final gesture she must say to the other players, "Thank you very much, ladies," without smiling, laughing, or appearing to gloat. If the departing player gives way to any of these expressions she must perform a suitable forfeit—such as standing on one leg until the next round is completed.

❋ If no one guesses correctly, everyone has a drink and a new round begins. With each new round, the first guess moves to the next player in sequence. The game continues, with player after player dropping out, until only one person is left. She is deemed the loser and has to make a round of drinks.

Silly Things to Do

Number of players: 10+

You will need: No special equipment.

How to play:

❊ The party host assembles everyone in a circle and ensures that each participant has a full glass of beer or soft drink. She then assigns to each person a particular action or task they have to perform nonstop while downing their drink.

❊ It helps to have the assignments worked out in advance so as not to delay things unduly.

❊ A few examples of the crazy things you could get the players to do:

- Continuously standing up and sitting down.
- Moving round the room on their knees.
- Crawling on all threes (the "fourth" will be needed to hold the glass).
- Balancing a pillow on the head.
- Miming an Egyptian belly dance.
- Performing a striptease.

❊ The host gives the signal to start and acts as referee, keeping an eye on everyone to see that the allotted tasks are being performed as specified.

❊ Anyone who stops either drinking or performing, or fails to perform her task correctly, has her glass topped up and must begin again.

❊ The winner is the first to empty her glass whilst faultlessly performing her own crazy assignment.

angelic delights

Non-alcoholic drinks are no longer the poor relations at a cocktail party. Once you've sampled the delights of these "virgin cocktails," you may never want to go back. Try a Kiwi Cooler, a Cherry Kiss, or a Summer Citrus Slush and see what you've been missing!

Nectarine Melt

serves 2 ⁂ 8 fl oz/225 ml milk ⁂ 12 oz/350 g lemon sherbet ⁂ 1 ripe mango, peeled, pitted, and diced ⁂ 2 ripe nectarines, peeled, pitted, and diced

This golden-yellow fruit smoothie, served icy cold, is very nourishing and is packed with vitamins, so you don't need to feel too guilty!

- Gently blend the milk with half the lemon sherbet until combined.
- Add the remaining sherbet and process until smooth.
- When the mixture is well blended, add the fruit and process until smooth.
- Pour into chilled glasses and drink with straws.

Kiwi Cooler

serves 1 ⁂ 1 ripe kiwi, peeled and crushed ⁂ crushed ice ⁂ juice of 1 passion fruit ⁂ splash of lime juice ⁂ lemonade ⁂ kiwi-filled ice cubes

You can only make this at the last minute, and it should be served almost frozen. Strain to remove the black seeds if they worry you!

- In a blender, quickly whizz the kiwi, ice, and passion fruit.
- Pour into a tall chilled glass, add a splash of lime juice, and top up with lemonade to taste.
- Finish with an ice cube with a piece of kiwi frozen inside it.

Muddy Puddle

serves 1 ⁑ juice of half a lemon ⁑ juice of half an orange ⁑ crushed ice ⁑ cola

to decorate ⁑ slice of orange

Is this one reminiscent of the mess your children make when mixing drinks? Well, in fact, that's just how this murky-looking but surprisingly refreshing drink was created.

- Pour the fruit juice over crushed ice in a tall chilled glass and top up with the well-iced cola.
- Finish with a slice of orange and serve with a straw.

Island Cooler

serves 1 ⁜ 2 measures orange juice ⁜ 1 measure lemon juice ⁜ 1 measure pineapple juice ⁜ 1 measure papaya juice ⁜ 1/2 tsp grenadine ⁜ cracked ice cubes ⁜ sparkling water

to decorate ⁜ pineapple and maraschino cherries on cocktail sticks

Nothing could be more refreshing on a hot summer's day than this colorful combination of tropical fruit juices. To get into a party mood, go to town with the decoration and lots of fresh fruit.

- Shake the orange juice, lemon juice, pineapple juice, papaya juice, and grenadine vigorously over ice until well frosted.
- Half fill a chilled Collins glass with cracked ice cubes and pour the cocktail over them.
- Top up with sparkling water and stir gently.
- Dress with pineapple and a maraschino cherry.

Grapefruit Cooler

serves 6 ⁂ 2 oz/55 g fresh mint ⁂ 2 measures sugar syrup ⁂ 1¼ pints/600 ml grapefruit juice ⁂ 4 measures lemon juice ⁂ cracked ice cubes ⁂ sparkling mineral water

to decorate ⁂ sprigs of fresh mint

Start making this wonderfully refreshing drink at least two hours before you want to serve it, to allow plenty of time for the mint to infuse in the syrup.

- Mash fresh mint leaves in a small bowl with the sugar syrup.
- Set aside for at least 2 hours to infuse, mashing again from time to time.
- Strain into a jug and add the grapefruit juice and lemon juice. Cover with plastic wrap and chill for at least 2 hours until required.
- To serve, fill six chilled Collins glasses with cracked ice.
- Divide the cocktail between the glasses and top up with sparkling water. Dress with fresh mint.

Summer Citrus Slush

serves 2 ⁂ 4 tbsp orange juice ⁂ 1 tbsp lime juice ⁂ 4 fl oz/125 ml sparkling water ⁂ 12 oz/350 g frozen summer fruits such as blueberries, raspberries, blackberries, and strawberries ⁂ 4 ice cubes

to decorate ⁂ selection of fresh berries

This is a great cocktail for a group of friends spending an afternoon at a summer garden party.

- Pour the orange juice, lime juice, and sparkling water into a food processor and process gently until mixed.
- Add the summer fruits and ice cubes and process until slushy.
- Pour the mixture into chilled glasses and dress with fresh berries.

Pineapple Crush

serves 2 ⁜ 4 fl oz/125 ml pineapple juice ⁜ 4 tbsp orange juice ⁜ 4 oz/115 g galia melon, cut into chunks ⁜ 5 oz/140 g frozen pineapple chunks ⁜ 4 ice cubes

to decorate ⁜ thin slices of fresh galia melon and orange peel

The more iced these ingredients are, the nicer the result will be, so plan ahead to give yourself at least 1 hour to chill everything first.

- Pour the ingredients into a food processor and process quickly until slushy.
- Pour straight into well-chilled tumblers and top with the fruit.

Cherry Kiss

serves 2 ⁑ 8 ice cubes, crushed ⁑ 2 tbsp cherry syrup ⁑ 2–3 splashes fresh lime juice ⁑ 1¼ pints/600 ml sparkling water

to decorate ⁑ maraschino cherries on cocktail sticks

A refreshing and almost calorie-free cocktail that is perfect for dieting, or simply for one of those no-alcohol occasions.

- Divide the crushed ice between two glasses and pour the syrup over.
- Add the lime juice and top up with sparkling water.
- Decorate with the maraschino cherries and serve.

Lemon Soda

serves 6 ⁜ 8 large lemons ⁜ 7 oz/200 g superfine sugar, plus extra to taste ⁜ 6 fl oz/175 ml boiling water ⁜ ice ⁜ soda water

to decorate ⁜ twist of lemon

You certainly get the very best and freshest lemony flavor by squeezing your own fresh lemon juice. This can be bottled and kept in the refrigerator for a few days.

- Finely grate the peel and squeeze the juice of 7 lemons into a large heatproof bowl.
- Thinly slice the remaining lemon and reserve for serving.
- Stir sugar and boiling water into the lemon juice and chill until required.
- To serve, strain into a pitcher with ice and dilute with soda water to taste.
- Add extra sugar, if desired. Serve in chilled glasses, dressed with lemon slices.

Faux Kir

serves 1 ⁜ 1 measure chilled raspberry syrup ⁜ chilled white grape juice

A non-alcoholic version of the classic wine cocktail, this drink is just as colorful and tasty. French and Italian fruit syrups are often the best quality and have the most flavor.

- Pour the raspberry syrup into a chilled wine glass.
- Top up with the grape juice.
- Stir well to mix.

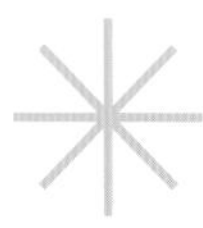

Strawberry and Pineapple Refresher

serves 2 ⁘ 6 oz/175 g frozen strawberries ⁘ 10 fl oz/300 ml long-life pineapple juice ⁘ 1 tbsp superfine sugar

Long life pineapple juice and frozen fruit are used in this easy-to-assemble smoothie made with pantry ingredients—the flavors are not compromised by your haste!

- Put the strawberries, pineapple juice, and sugar into a food processor and blend until smooth.
- Pour into glasses and serve at once.

Raspberry Lemonade

serves 4 ⁜ 2 lemons ⁜ 4 oz/115 g superfine sugar ⁜ 4 oz/115 g fresh raspberries ⁜ few drops vanilla essence ⁜ crushed ice ⁜ sparkling water, iced

to decorate ⁜ sprigs of lemon balm

If you like real old-fashioned lemonade, you will love this version.

- Trim the ends off the lemons, scoop out and chop the flesh, and place in a blender with the sugar, raspberries, vanilla, and ice.
- Blend for 2–3 minutes or until there are no lumps.
- Strain into tall glasses and top up with ice cubes and water. Finish with sprigs of lemon balm.

Drinking Games

Name Dropping

Number of players: 4–10

You will need: No special equipment.

How to play:

❋ Most of us are guilty of name dropping once in a while. Now you have the chance to drop all the names you like with a clear conscience.

❋ Someone gets the game under way by saying the name of a famous living person. Moving clockwise, the next player has to come up with a famous name starting with the first letter of the previous candidate's last name. And so the game continues, player after player.

❋ For example: Jennifer Aniston = Angelina Jolie = Jamie Lee Curtis = Christina Ricci = Renée Zellwegger = Zsa Zsa Gabor...

❋ If a player fails to come up with a name after no more than a few moments' thought, or submits an incorrect name she must have a drink and the game moves on at once to the next player. If someone thinks of a celebrity whose first and last names begin with the same letter (e.g. Robert Redford), everyone has a drink except the player in question.

❋ Single-name celebrities such as Cher, Madonna, or Sting are not acceptable and, if nominated, count as a mistake—though they shouldn't take it personally!

Who Said That?

Number of players: 6+

You will need: No special equipment.

How to play:

❊ The object of the game is to put the name of a famous person or fictional character to certain well-known catchphrases.

❊ The player who begins recites a catchphrase and then challenges a member of the group to come up with the name of the person who said it. Any player can be chosen to respond, but no one can be selected twice in a row.

❊ If the catchphrase comes from a movie or TV program, the respondent must give the name of the character, the actor, and the film or show title. If it comes from a book, the answer must include title, author, and character's name.

❊ If a player comes up with the correct answer, the questioner must have a drink. If the player answers incorrectly or not in full she must have a drink. If the questioner misquotes the phrase she incurs a two-drink penalty.

❊ The game moves clockwise round the circle, each player taking it in turn to deliver a catchphrase and say, "Who said that?" You can prepare a few catchphrases before the game begins or rely on players to come up with their favorite lines on the spot.

❊ Here are some examples:

"Heeeeerre's Johnny!" (Johnny Carson)

"Howya doin'?" (Joey/Matt Le Blanc, *Friends*)

"Read my lips—no new taxes." (George Bush Snr)

"I shall return." (General Douglas MacArthur)

"Come up and see me some time." (Mae West)

Scissors, Paper, Stone

Number of players: 4+

You will need: No special equipment.

How to play:

❉ A drinking version of the traditional playground game in which a bunched fist = a stone, two fingers parted wide = scissors, and a flat hand = a sheet of paper.

❉ Scissors can cut paper but are blunted by a stone. Paper can wrap around a stone but is cut by scissors. A stone can blunt scissors but is wrapped in paper.

❉ The players sit on opposite sides of a table, with the first two to play facing each other. Keeping one hand out of sight beneath the table, each player adopts one of the above forms—stone, scissors, or paper. On the count of three, the two players simultaneously reveal their hands. The player with the losing hand has to down the contents of her glass, however much is in it, and the game moves on to the next facing pair.

❉ If neither hand wins—that is, if they both produce the same shape (e.g. a "stone")—both players have to have a drink and try again.

❉ And you thought you were no longer a kid!

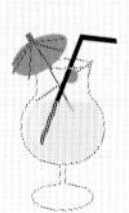

Z to A

Number of players: 3+

You will need: No special equipment.

How to play:

✻ To be said to know the alphabet backward is a common expression. But how many people actually do know their Z through to A?

✻ The aim is to recite the English alphabet backward without undue hesitation and without making a mistake. If a player pauses for too long between letters or makes an error, she must have a drink, go back to Z, and start over. After three such faults, the player is ruled out and incurs an additional two-drink penalty. The alphabet challenge then passes to the next player.

fine finales

For the perfect end to a classic cocktail party, you need a grand finale. Providing after-dinner (or after-party) drinks at the end of the evening oozes sophistication. Offer your guests an Irish Coffee, Rum Toddy, or a Port and Lemon Mull and they'll be forever grateful.

Spiced Hot Chocolate

serves 4 ⁘ $2\frac{1}{4}$ pints/1 liter milk ⁘ 7 oz/200 g semisweet chocolate (at least 70 percent cocoa solids) broken into small pieces ⁘ 2 tsp superfine sugar ⁘ 1 tsp mixed spice

to decorate ⁘ 2 tbsp whipped cream ⁘ 4 sticks cinnamon

This is a seriously good version of hot chocolate, not for everyday but perhaps as a treat.

- Put the milk, chocolate, sugar, and mixed spice into a pan over medium heat.
- Whisk, stirring constantly, until the chocolate has melted and the mixture is simmering but not boiling.
- Remove from the heat and pour into heatproof glasses or cups.
- Top with a little whipped cream and decorate with cinnamon sticks.

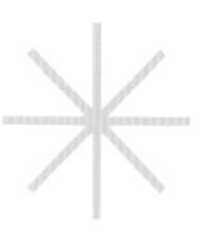

Port & Lemon Mull

serves 10 ⁜ few cloves ⁜ 2 lemons ⁜ 1 bottle port ⁜ 1 1/4 pints/600 ml boiling water ⁜ mixed spices ⁜ 2 oz/55 g sugar cubes

The clove-studded lemon in this recipe is a very successful old-fashioned way of flavoring warm wine or port.

- Push the cloves into 1 lemon and warm in a medium oven for 15 minutes.
- Pour the port into a medium-large pan, bring just to scalding and turn off. Boil the water and add a pinch of mixed spices to it.
- Cut the other lemon in half and squeeze out half the juice.
- Add everything to the pan of port and heat to dissolve the sugar.
- Remove the cloved lemon before serving. Serve really hot in small heatproof glasses or cups.

Toasted Almonds

serves 1 ⁜ 2 ice cubes ⁜ 2 measures Amaretto ⁜ 1 measure brandy ⁜ 1–2 measures heavy cream

to decorate ⁜ toasted slivered almonds

You can't beat this for a wonderfully rich after-dinner treat. Serve with candied almonds for a good effect.

- Place 2 ice cubes in a chilled cocktail glass.
- Stir in the Amaretto and brandy to mix well and chill.
- With the help of a spoon, pour the cream in a layer over the top and finish with a few toasted slivered almonds.

Toasted Almonds

serves 1 ⁂ 2 ice cubes ⁂ 2 measures Amaretto ⁂ 1 measure brandy ⁂ 1–2 measures heavy cream

to decorate ⁂ toasted slivered almonds

You can't beat this for a wonderfully rich after-dinner treat. Serve with candied almonds for a good effect.

- Place 2 ice cubes in a chilled cocktail glass.
- Stir in the Amaretto and brandy to mix well and chill.
- With the help of a spoon, pour the cream in a layer over the top and finish with a few toasted slivered almonds.

Irish Coffee

serves 1 ⁜ 2 measures Irish whiskey ⁜ sugar to taste ⁜ freshly brewed strong black coffee ⁜ 2 measures heavy cream

This is thought to have been created by Joe Sheridan in the 1940s when he was head chef at Shannon Airport, Ireland.

- Put the whiskey into a warmed heatproof glass with sugar to taste.
- Pour in the coffee and stir.
- When the sugar has completely dissolved, pour the cream very slowly over the back of a spoon which is just touching the top of the coffee and the edge of the glass.
- Keep pouring until all the cream has been added and has settled on the top.
- Do not stir, but drink the coffee through the cream.

Springbok Coffee

serves 1 ⁜ 8 fl oz/225 ml strong black coffee ⁜ 1 measure apricot brandy ⁜ 1 measure Amarula

to decorate ⁜ whipped cream ⁜ toasted slivered almonds

A fruity but rather rich coffee to serve hot or iced.

- Pour the coffee into a tall heatproof glass or cup.
- Pour in the brandy and then carefully pour in the Amarula cream liqueur.
- Finish with a swirl of whipped cream and a few toasted slivered almonds.

Snowy Ridge

serves 1 ⁜ 1 measure crème de cacao, chilled ⁜ $\frac{1}{2}$ measure heavy cream

Cream-topped liqueurs are delicious after-dinner drinks. Any favorite can be used, but it works best with a well-chilled liqueur.

- Pour the crème de cacao into an iced shot glass or small cocktail glass.
- Carefully pour the cream over the back of a spoon on top of the liqueur so that it floats.
- Sip the liqueur slowly through the cream.

Coffee Time

serves 1 ⁜ 1 measure coconut liqueur ⁜ 1 measure coffee liqueur ⁜ 1 measure brandy
⁜ freshly brewed hot coffee

to decorate ⁜ whipped sweetened cream

This is a luxurious coffee for any after-dinner occasion. Have plenty ready, as it will go down very well.

- Mix the liqueurs and brandy in a heatproof glass or cup.
- Pour in the fresh coffee and top with a spoonful of whipped cream.

After Nine

serves 1 ⁜ 1 measure whiskey ⁜ 1 measure chocolate mint liqueur ⁜ 1 measure cream ⁜ ice

to decorate ⁜ grated chocolate

There is certainly no need to serve chocolate after dinner to anyone who is enjoying this rich cocktail.

- Briefly stir or whisk all the ingredients together with a little ice.
- Strain into a cocktail glass and sprinkle with grated chocolate.

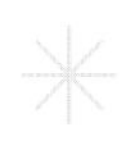

Jealousy

serves 1 ⁂ 1 tsp crème de menthe ⁂ 1–2 tbsp heavy cream ⁂ 2 measures coffee or chocolate liqueur ⁂ crushed ice

to decorate ⁂ chocolate sticks

This is a true after-dinner cocktail, and if you want a change you could occasionally flavor the cream with a different liqueur.

- Gently beat the mint liqueur into the cream until thick.
- Pour the coffee liqueur into a very small iced cocktail glass and carefully spoon on the whipped flavored cream.
- Serve with chocolate sticks.

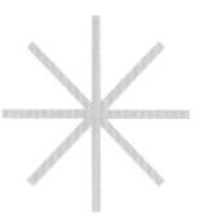

Mah Jong

serves 1 ⁘ 1 measure gin ⁘ ¼ measure Cointreau ⁘ ¼ measure white rum ⁘ ice

to decorate ⁘ strip of orange peel

No Chinese games here, but you may not be walking in perfect straight lines if you drink too many!

- Stir all the ingredients over ice in a mixing glass and strain into a chilled small cocktail glass.
- Dress with a piece of orange peel.

Rum Toddy

serves 1 ⁑ 1 measure dark rum ⁑ 1 measure water ⁑ sugar to taste

to decorate ⁑ twist of orange peel

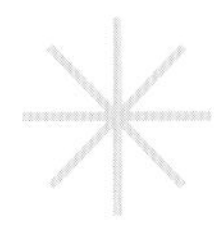

This winter drink tastes just as good using brandy instead of rum, but be prepared—warming the alcohol always seems to make it stronger.

- Warm the rum with the water and add sugar to taste.
- Add the orange peel and serve in a heatproof glass or cup.

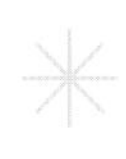

Jagger Tae

serves 1 ⁂ hot fresh tea without milk ⁂ sugar to taste ⁂ 2–3 measures schnapps or brandy

to decorate ⁂ slice of lemon

This tea-based cocktail makes a refreshing change from the many coffee-based after-dinner drinks.

- Pour the hot tea into a heated glass or cup, add sugar to taste, and stir until it has dissolved.
- Add the schnapps and finish with a slice of lemon. Serve very hot.

Chocolate Cream Fizz

serves 1 ⁜ 1 measure white rum ⁜ $^1/_2$ measure chocolate mint liqueur ⁜ generous dash of crème de menthe ⁜ dash lemon juice ⁜ scoop chocolate mint ice cream ⁜ soda water

to decorate ⁜ flaked white chocolate

This is a seriously rich version of a fizz with ice cream added—it's certainly not for dieters!

- In a blender on slow speed, whizz all the ingredients except the soda water.
- Pour into an iced glass, top up with soda water to fizz, and serve with flaked white chocolate.

Chocolate Egg Nog

serves 8 ⁜ 8 egg yolks ⁜ 7 oz/200 g sugar ⁜ $2^1/_2$ pints/1.2 liters milk
⁜ 8 oz/225 g semisweet chocolate, grated ⁜ 6 measures dark rum

The perfect pick-me-up on a cold winter's night, this delicious drink will get the taste buds tingling.

- Beat the egg yolks with the sugar until thickened.
- Pour the milk into a large pan, add the grated chocolate, and bring just to a boil.
- Remove from the heat and gradually beat in the egg yolk mixture.
- Stir in the rum and pour into heatproof glasses or cups.

Drinking Games

Chef's Menu

Number of players: 6+

You will need: No special equipment.

How to play:

❋ This is just the game to play after consuming a large meal and downing a few drinks.

❋ One of the group takes on the role of chef. She then selects one of the other players and challenges them to come up with five items of food for the menu, each beginning with the same letter.

❋ For example:

Chef: "For my menu today I want to cook with food beginning with the letter 'T.'"

❋ **Player one:** "Tomatoes, tuna, turkey, tarragon, turnips."

❋ The food item must be an ingredient or a generic type; cooked dishes such as Chicken Pot Pie or Baked Alaska are not allowed.

❋ If the player comes up with five correct items, the chef must have a drink and the player takes over the role of chef.

❋ For every item they fail to come up with, or for every one that is incorrect, the player incurs a drink penalty—e.g. only three correct answers means having two drinks.

❋ Start off with the easier letters to get the game under way. When it gets to Q, X, and Z, the drinking rate increases significantly!

Celebrity Links

Number of players: 6+

You will need: No special equipment.

How to play:

❋ How well do you know the professional and private lives of celebrities?

❋ The first player names a celebrity. The next player has to come up with another celebrity who is in some way associated with the first one. The third player adds another celebrity link, and so on round the circle.

❋ For example:

Player one:	Katie Holmes
Player two:	Tom Cruise
Player three:	Nicole Kidman
Player four:	Sean Penn
Player five:	Clint Eastwood
Player six:	Hilary Swank

❋ If a player fails to come up with the name of a celebrity, she must have a drink and the next player continues the game. A "celebrity link" can be challenged by any of the other players who can demand to know precisely what the association is. If the player challenged gives a satisfactory explanation, the challenger must have a drink. If the player fails to establish a credible link, the penalty incurred is two drinks and the play passes to the next player.

❋ Players can also be "timed out" (i.e. obliged to take a drink) for taking too long to conjure up a celebrity name.

21

Number of players: 4+

You will need: A deck of cards.

How to play:

✲ The players take it in turns to be the dealer. Two cards are dealt to each player, face down. The object is to score 21 or as close as you can get to it without going bust (i.e. over 21). Extra cards are dealt, one at a time, on request. Aces count as 11 and all picture cards as 10.

✲ If any player achieves a score of 21, the dealer must have a drink. If a player goes bust she must have a drink. If no one gets 21 or goes bust, all those except the person with the highest score must have a drink.

Truth or Dare

Number of players: 4+

You will need: No special equipment.

How to play:

❋ Each player in turn has to make the choice between answering a question truthfully or performing a dare. Needless to say, the questions are likely to be very personal and the dares very daring. The game moves clockwise around the group, with each player challenging the person on her left.

❋ A person can decline to choose either the truth or dare option by electing instead to down the contents of her glass, but it is more fun for all concerned if everyone takes part. A word of warning: don't ask questions that are going to hurt or acutely embarrass anyone or challenge anyone to carry out a dare that is in any way dangerous.

❋ If a player responds to a question less than truthfully or fails to complete her dare, it's a two-drink penalty.

Index